Viola Time Jog

T0083052

a first book of very easy pieces for viola

Kathy and David Blackwell

Illustrations by

Martin Remphry

Welcome to the third edition of ***Viola Time Joggers***. You'll find:

- open string pieces and tunes using the finger pattern 0–1–23–4
- duets—start with the staves marked ☆; come back and play the other part later!
- three new pieces, replacing nos. 3 and 29 and ensemble part no. 44
- audio play-along tracks available to download from www.oup.com/vtjoggers3e or to access on principal streaming platforms
- piano and viola accompaniments available separately in printed collections
- an ideal book to use alongside *Viola Time Starters*
- a book for viola that's also compatible with *Fiddle Time Joggers*

Teacher's note:

Forty-four of the 47 tunes from *Fiddle Time Joggers* are compatible with *Viola Time Joggers*. In a few pieces, some details are different between the two books, for example some bar numbers and introductions.

denotes a part that fits with *Fiddle Time Joggers*: these are printed in sequence in the book or on pages 32–5. In audio tracks 51–9, the part is played first by viola and piano, and then with the violin part added.

C string special denotes pieces that provide practice on the C string.

1 indicates the audio track number; it is given only where a piece number and its corresponding audio track number differ.

OXFORD
UNIVERSITY PRESS

OXFORD
UNIVERSITY PRESS

Great Clarendon Street, Oxford OX2 6DP, England

Oxford University Press is a department of the University of Oxford.
It furthers the University's aim of excellence in research, scholarship,
and education by publishing worldwide

Oxford is a registered trade mark of Oxford University Press
in the UK and in certain other countries

This collection © Oxford University Press 2005, 2013, and 2022

Kathy and David Blackwell have asserted their right under the Copyright, Designs
and Patents Act, 1988, to be identified as the Composers of this Work

Database right Oxford University Press (maker)

First published 2005. Reprinted with corrections 2013 and with amendments 2022

All rights reserved. No part of this publication may be reproduced,
stored in a retrieval system, or transmitted, in any form or by any means,
without the prior permission in writing of Oxford University Press

Permission to perform this work in public (except in the course of divine
worship) should normally be obtained from a local performing right
licensing organization, unless the owner or the occupier of the premises being
used already holds a licence from such an organization. Likewise, permission to
make and exploit a recording of this work should be obtained from a local
mechanical copyright licensing organization

Enquiries concerning reproduction outside the scope of the above
should be directed to the Music Rights Department, Oxford University Press,
at music.permissions.uk@oup.com or at the address above

ISBN 978-0-19-356215-8

Music and text origination by Julia Bovee
Printed in Great Britain on acid-free paper by
Halstan & Co Ltd., Amersham, Bucks.

Unless otherwise marked, all pieces are by Kathy and David Blackwell and are
© Oxford University Press. All traditional pieces are arranged by Kathy and
David Blackwell and are © Oxford University Press. Unauthorized
arrangement or photocopying of this copyright material is ILLEGAL.

Contents

Open strings and first finger

1. Bow down, O Belinda (*duet*) 5
2. Under arrest! 5
3. Someone plucks, someone bows (*duet*) 6
4. Down up 6
5. Two in a boat (*duet*) 7
6. London Bridge (*duet*) 7
7. Fast lane 8
8. In flight 8
9. Lift off! 9
10. Katie's waltz 9
11. Copy cat (*duet*) 10
12. Tap dancer 11
13. Rhythm fever 11
14. Here it comes! 12
15. So there! 12
16. Rowing boat 13
17. Ally bally (*duet*) 13
18. Tiptoe, boo! 14
19. Travellin' slow 14
20. C string boogie 14

Second finger

21. Off to Paris (*duet*) 15
22. Clare's song 16
23. City lights 16
24. Daydream 17
25. On the prowl 17
26. Summer sun 18
27. Phoebe in her petticoat (*duet*) 18
28. Ready, steady, go now! 19
29. Cooking in the kitchen (*duet*) 19
30. Happy go lucky 20
31. The mocking bird (*duet*) 21

Third and fourth fingers

32. Algy met a bear (*duet*) 22
33. Listen to the rhythm 23
34. Cattle ranch blues 24
35. In the groove 24
36. Stamping dance 25
37. Distant bells 25
38. Lazy scale 26
39. Runaway train 26
40. Rocking horse 27
41. Patrick's reel 27
42. Calypso time 28
43. Tudor tune 28
44. Chopsticks for two (*duet*) 29
45. Carrion crow (*duet*) 30
46. Flying high 31
47. Viola Time 31

Ensemble parts—these are compatible with, and are numbered as, the pieces in *Fiddle Time Joggers*

20. Lazy cowboy 32
24. The three friends (*duet*) 32
25. Peace garden 32
35. In the groove 33
39. The old castle 33
42. Calypso time 34
44. Rocky mountain (*duet*) 34
45. Carrion crow (*duet*) 35
47. Fiddle Time 35

Music Fact-Finder Page 36

Open strings

C G D A

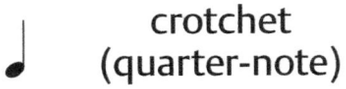

crotchet
(quarter-note)

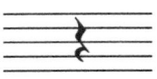

crotchet rest
(quarter-note rest)

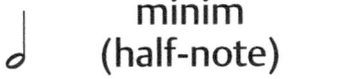

minim
(half-note)

minim rest
(half-note rest)

dotted minim
(dotted half-note)

1st finger

C D

G A

D E

A B

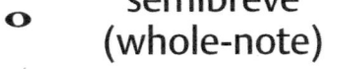

semibreve
(whole-note)

semibreve rest
(whole-note rest)
or whole bar rest
(whole measure rest)

1. Bow down, O Belinda

American folk tune

2. Under arrest!

KB & DB

Count 2 bars

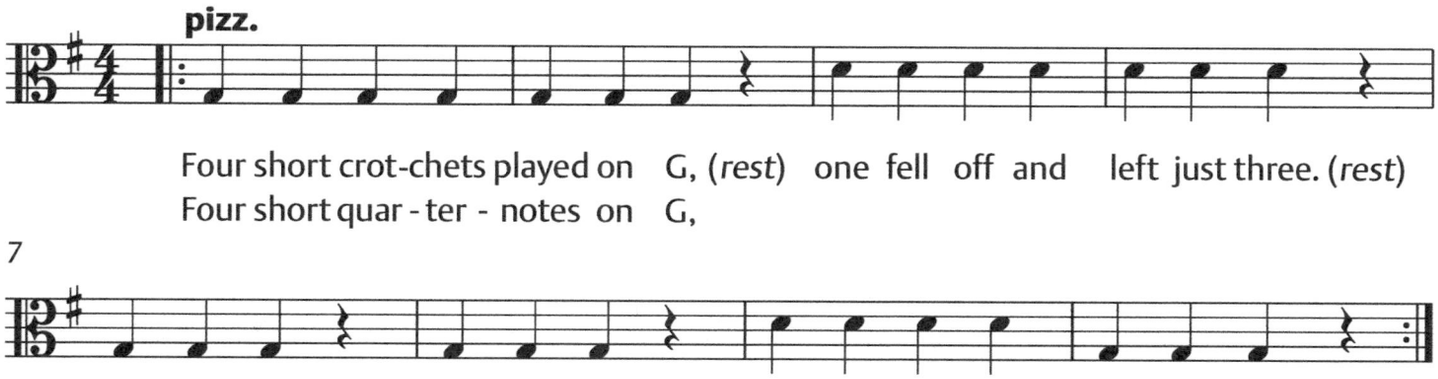

Four short crot-chets played on G, (*rest*) one fell off and left just three. (*rest*)
Four short quar - ter - notes on G,

1 2 3, (*rest*) 1 2 3, (*rest*) one fell off and left just three. (*rest*)

Say the word '*rest*' quietly to yourself as you play.

3. Someone plucks, someone bows

Traditional
Words KB & DB

3. *Someone plucks, someone bows*
(lower part of violin duet)

4. Down up

C string special

KB & DB

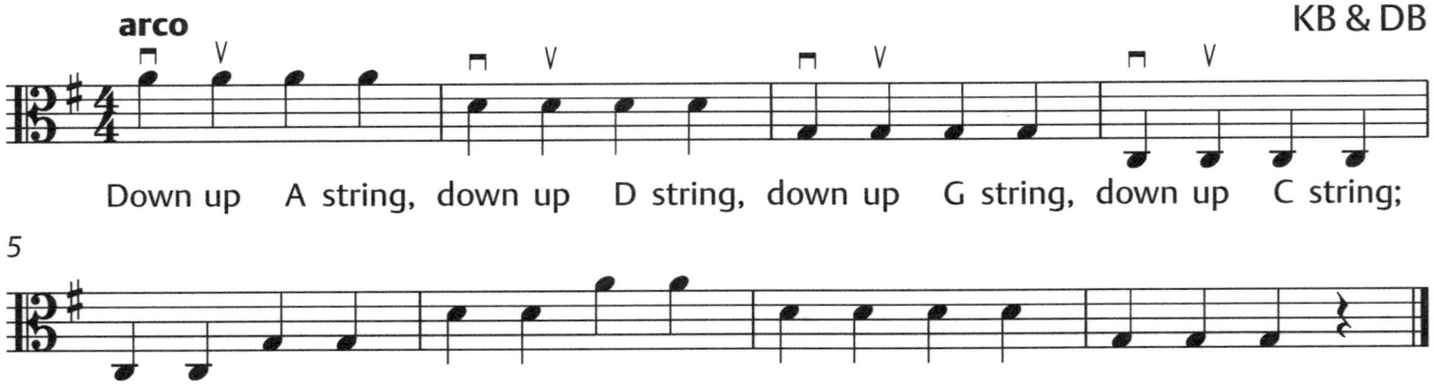

* [ ] Play the D and end with G.

* Fill in the letter names of these notes.

(No. 4 is not compatible with *Fiddle Time Joggers*.)

5. *Two in a boat*

American folk tune

49

5. *Two in a boat*
(lower part of violin duet)

6. *London Bridge*

English folk tune

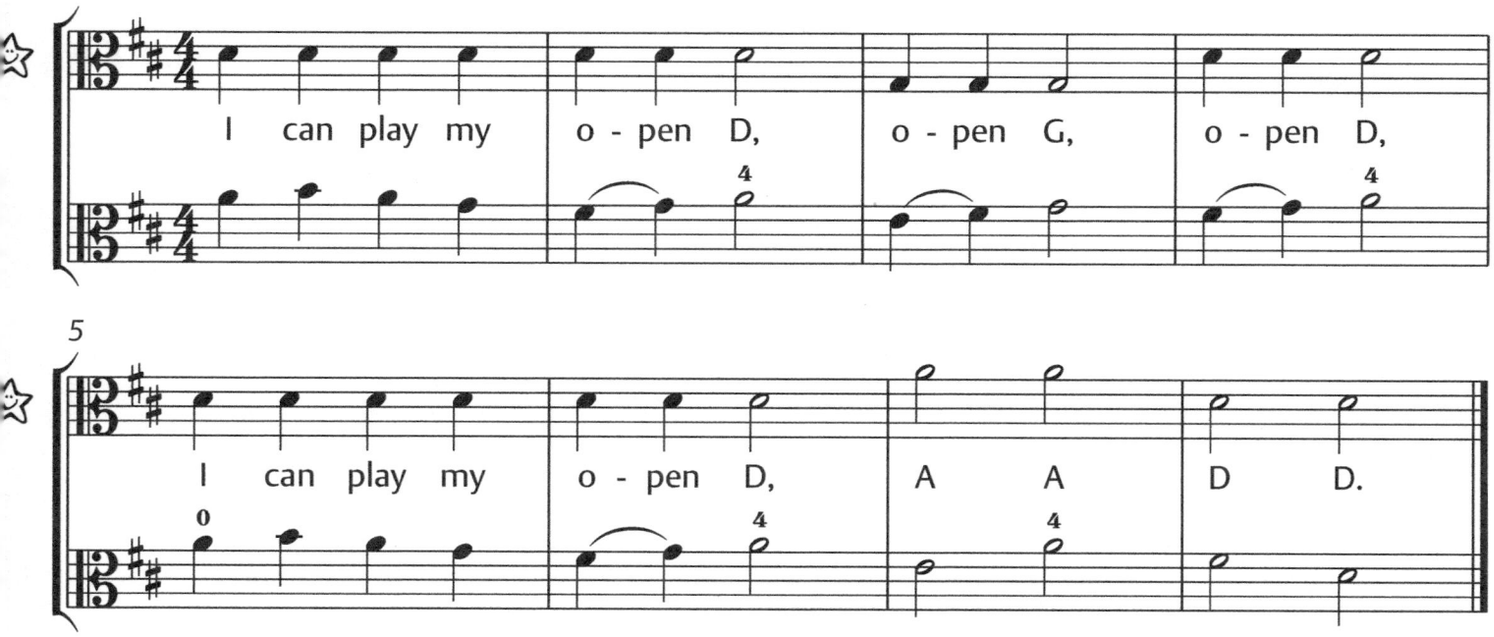

7. *Fast lane*

KB & DB

Try even faster the second time through!

8. *In flight*

KB & DB

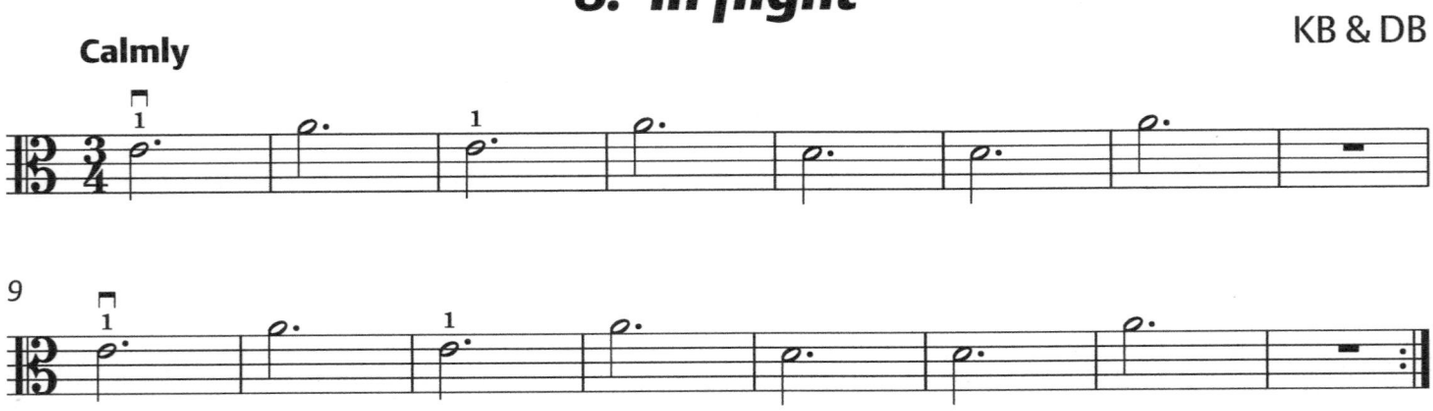

In the rests, let your bow make a circle as you swoop and soar like a bird.

9. Lift off!

KB & DB

Rock

Lift your bow off in each of the rests and let it orbit! (Make a circle with your right arm.)

Rhythm game:

Or - bit round the moon. (*etc.*)

10. Katie's waltz

Count 4 bars

KB & DB

Gently

11. Copy cat

KB & DB

12. Tap dancer

KB & DB

* Hold the bow upright and tap the screw end of the bow on your music stand.

13. Rhythm fever

Count 2 bars

KB & DB

14. Here it comes!

(adapted melody)

KB & DB

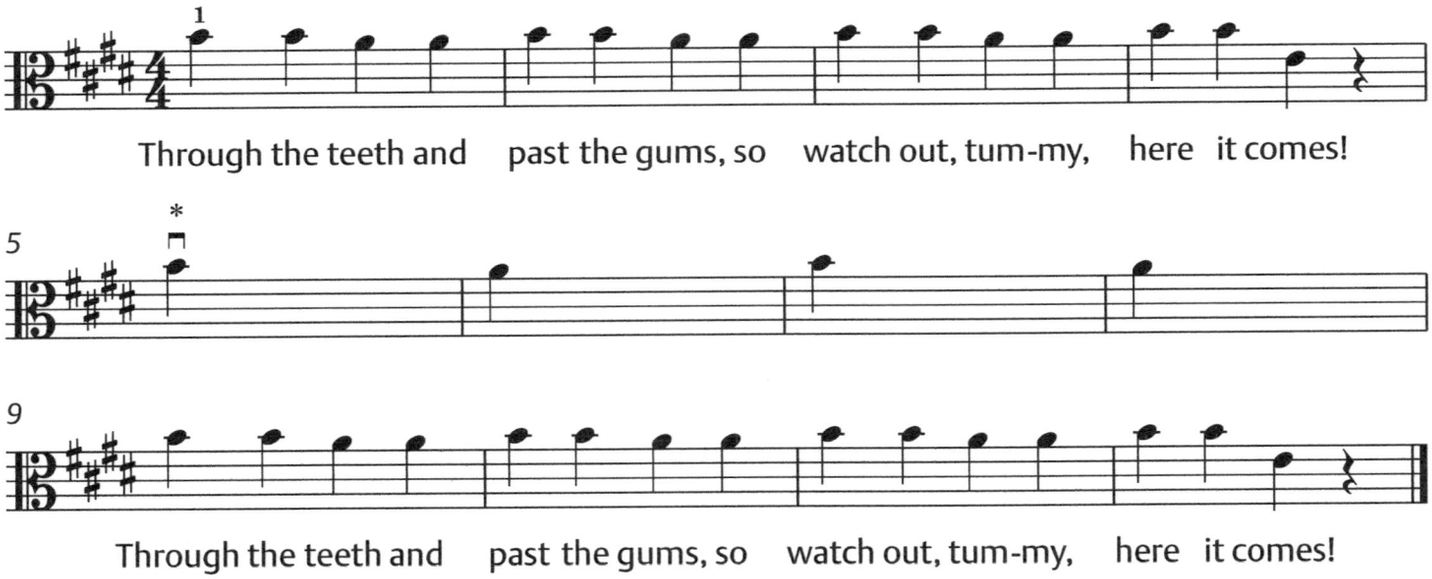

* Think of a foody rhythm and play it on these notes.

Here is an idea to start you off:

Fish and chips and ice cream.

15. So there!

(adapted melody)

KB & DB

Count 4 bars

Brightly

16. *Rowing boat*

KB & DB

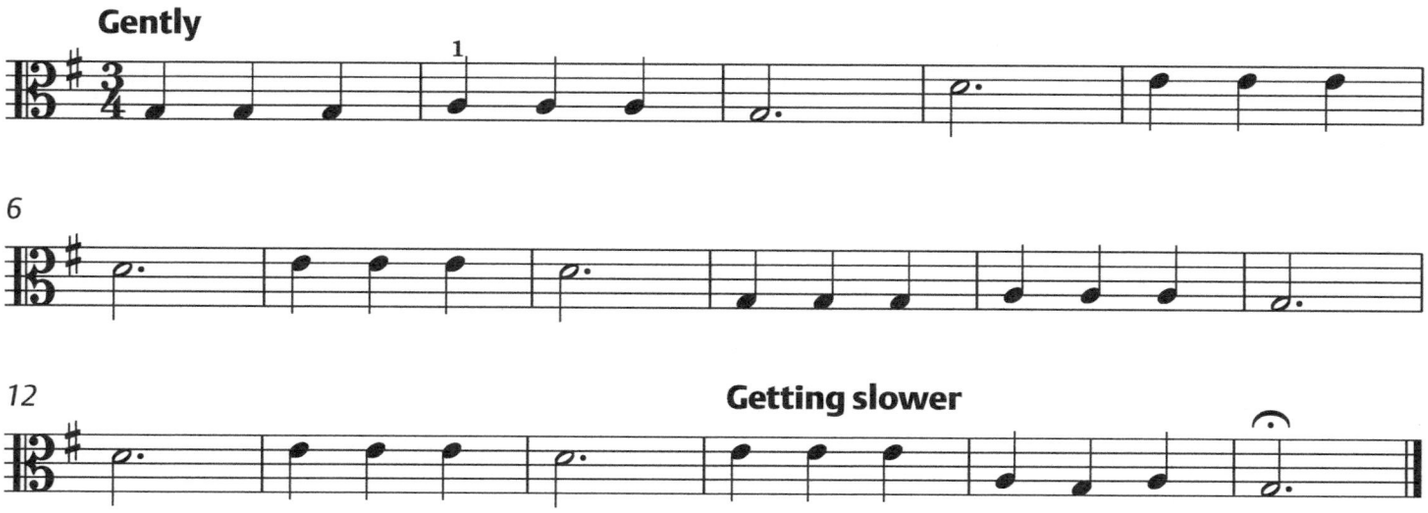

17. *Ally bally*

Scottish folk tune

17. *Ally bally*
(lower part of violin duet)

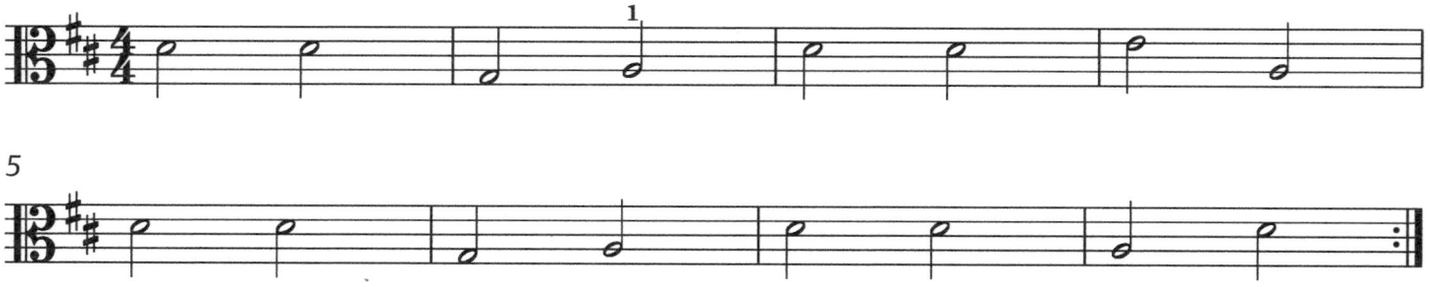

Count 2 bars

18. Tiptoe, boo!

KB & DB

Spookily!

Tip-toe tip-toe tip-toe, boo! (*etc.*)

9

15

21

Boo!
(shout!)

Also try playing this pizzicato.

19. Travellin' slow

KB & DB

In first gear

9

20. C string boogie

C string special

KB & DB

With a gentle swing
pizz.

1

7

*

13

* Turn around or, if you are sitting, stand up and sit down again!

20. Lazy cowboy—see page 32.

2nd finger

C D E

G A B

D E F♯

A B C♯

quavers
(eighth-notes)

21. Off to Paris

French folk tune

22. Clare's song

Count 4 bars

KB & DB

23. City lights

KB & DB

24. Daydream

C string special

Count 2 bars

KB & DB

24. The three friends—see page 32.

25. On the prowl

C string special

KB & DB

25. Peace garden—see page 32.

26. Summer sun

KB & DB

From now on, you'll be able to play both parts of the duets.

27. Phoebe in her petticoat

American folk tune

Swap parts when you do the repeat.

28. Ready, steady, go now!

(adapted melody)

KB & DB

Shout loudly and rhythmically before you start:

29. Cooking in the kitchen

KB & DB

30. *Happy go lucky* (for Iain)

Count 4 bars

KB & DB

Sunnily

f

11

mf

17

f

23

29

ff

31. The mocking bird

American folk tune

Now you can play the harder part of 'Someone plucks, someone bows' on page 6.

3rd and 4th fingers

slur

32. Algy met a bear

KB & DB
Words anon.

mf

Al - gy met a bear, a bear met Al - gy. The

mf

bear was bul - gy, the bulge was Al - gy!

Swap parts when you do the repeat.

33. Listen to the rhythm

Count 4 bars

KB & DB

34. Cattle ranch blues

KB & DB

Stompy

mf

5

cresc.

9

rit.

f

35. In the groove

Count 2 bars

KB & DB

Swing

mf cresc.

7

f

11

mf cresc.

15

f

20

rit.

mp

Now go back to page 15 and play the harder part of 'Off to Paris'.

35. In the groove—see page 33.

36. Stamping dance

Czech folk tune

Try the harder part of 'Bow down, O Belinda' on page 5.

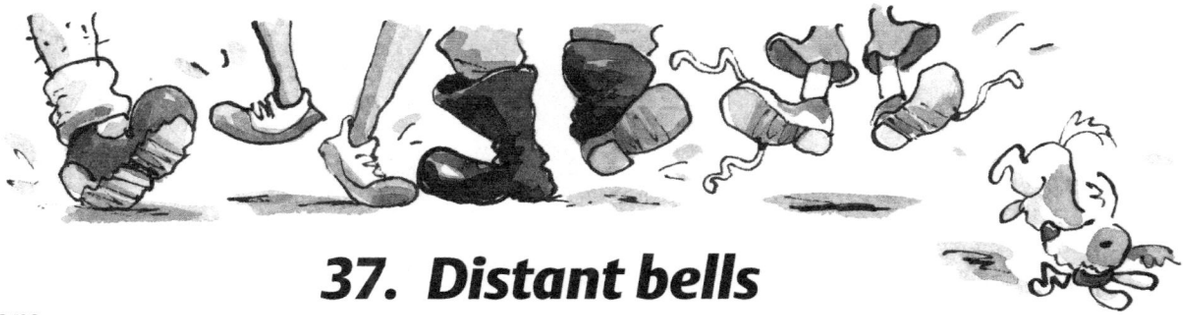

37. Distant bells

Count 2 bars

KB & DB

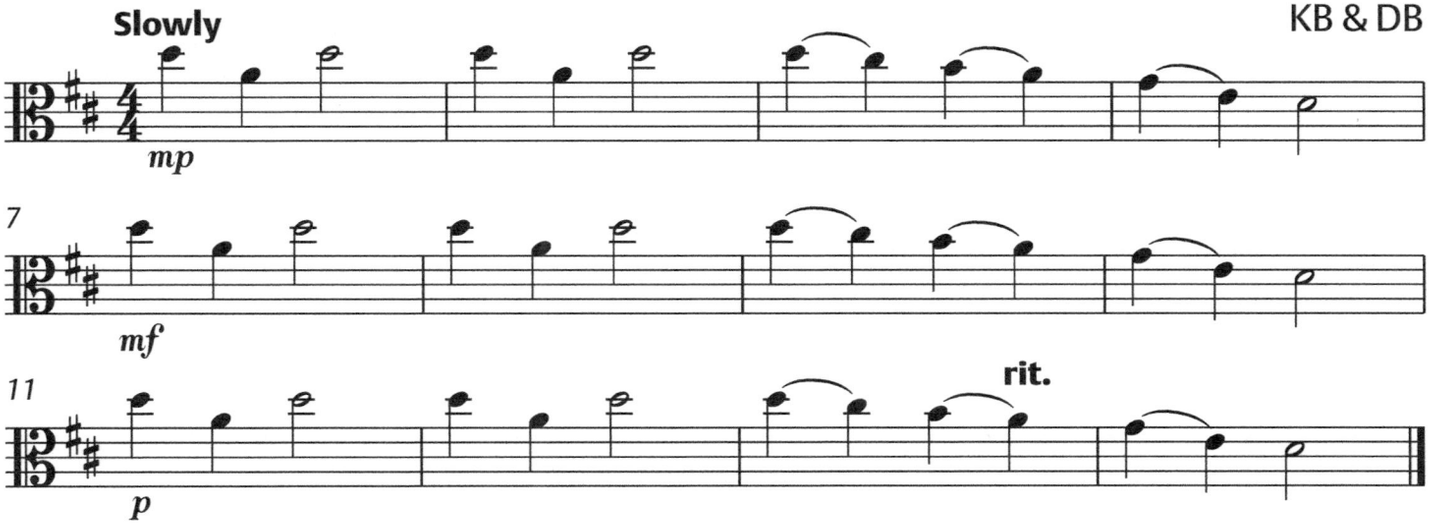

Now go back to page 16 and play 'Clare's song', slurring three crotchets (quarter-notes) to a bow.

38. Lazy scale

KB & DB

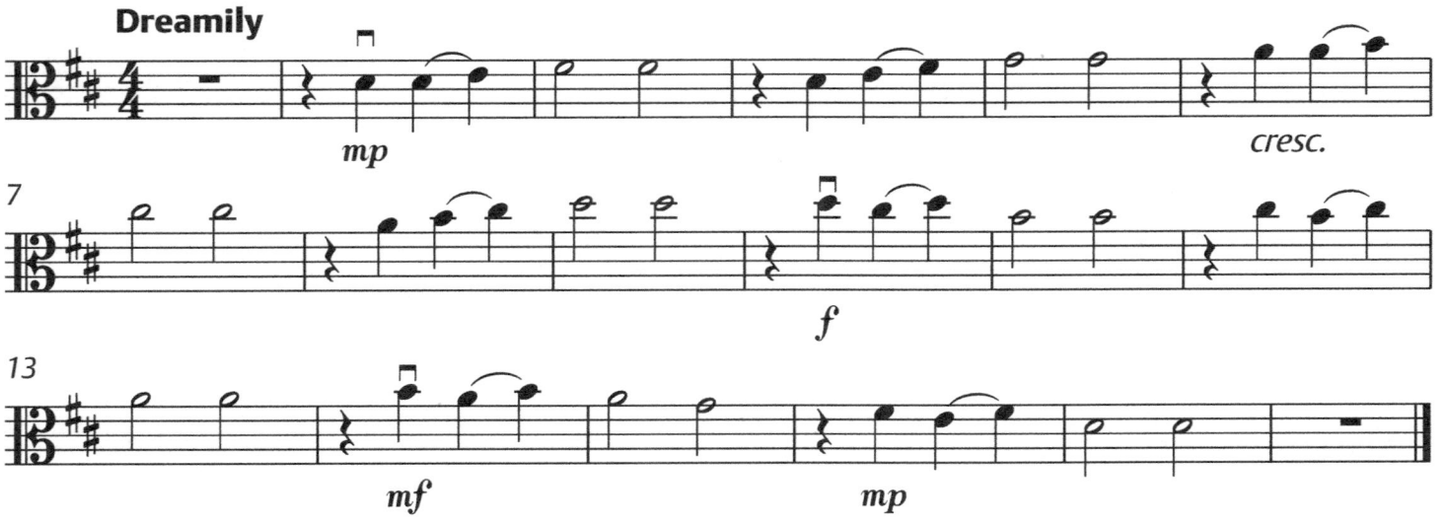

39. Runaway train

C string special

Count 4 bars

KB & DB

39. *The old castle*—see page 33.

40. Rocking horse

Count 4 bars

KB & DB

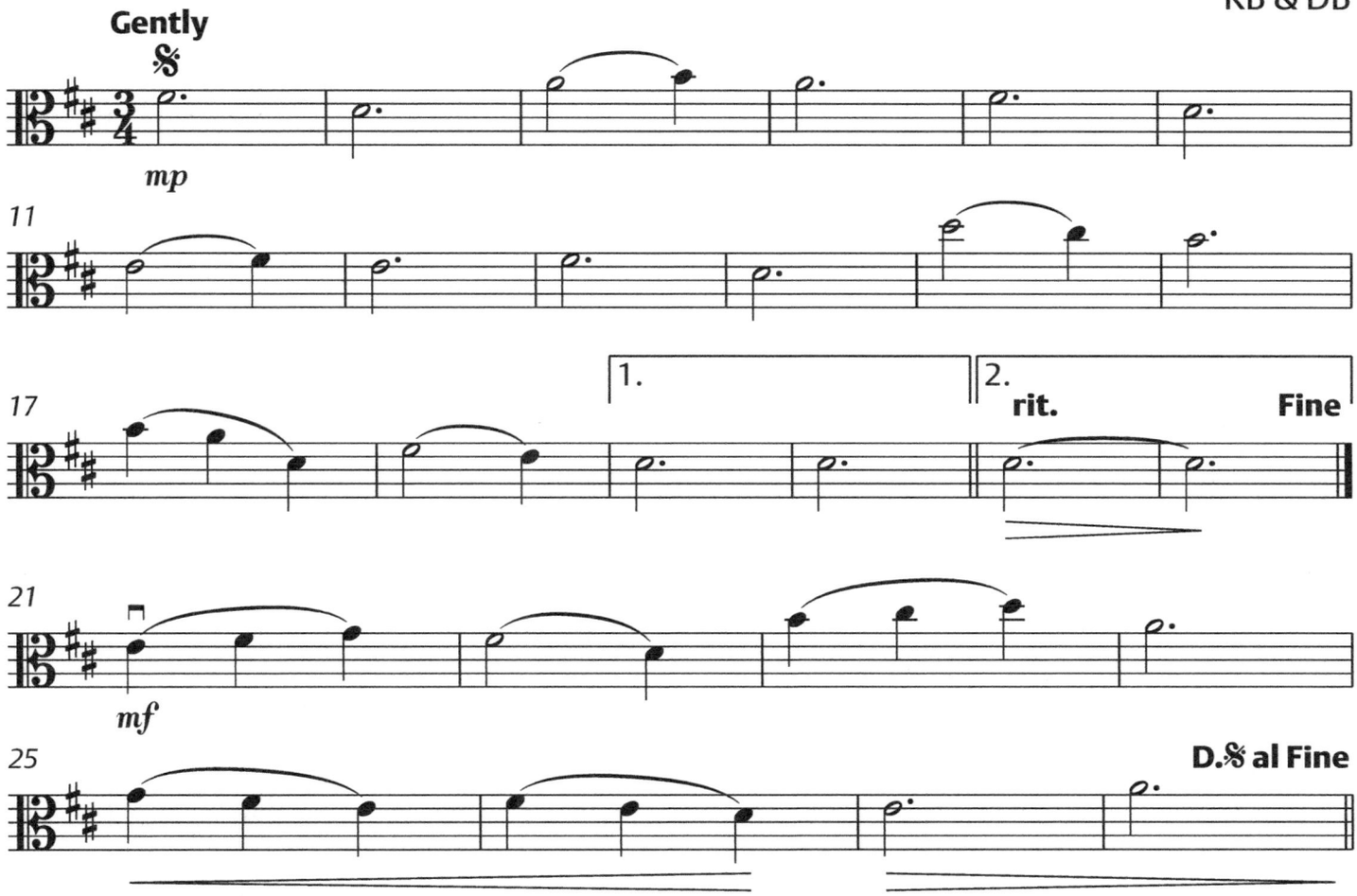

41. Patrick's reel

Count 2 bars

KB & DB

42. Calypso time

Count 2 bars

KB & DB

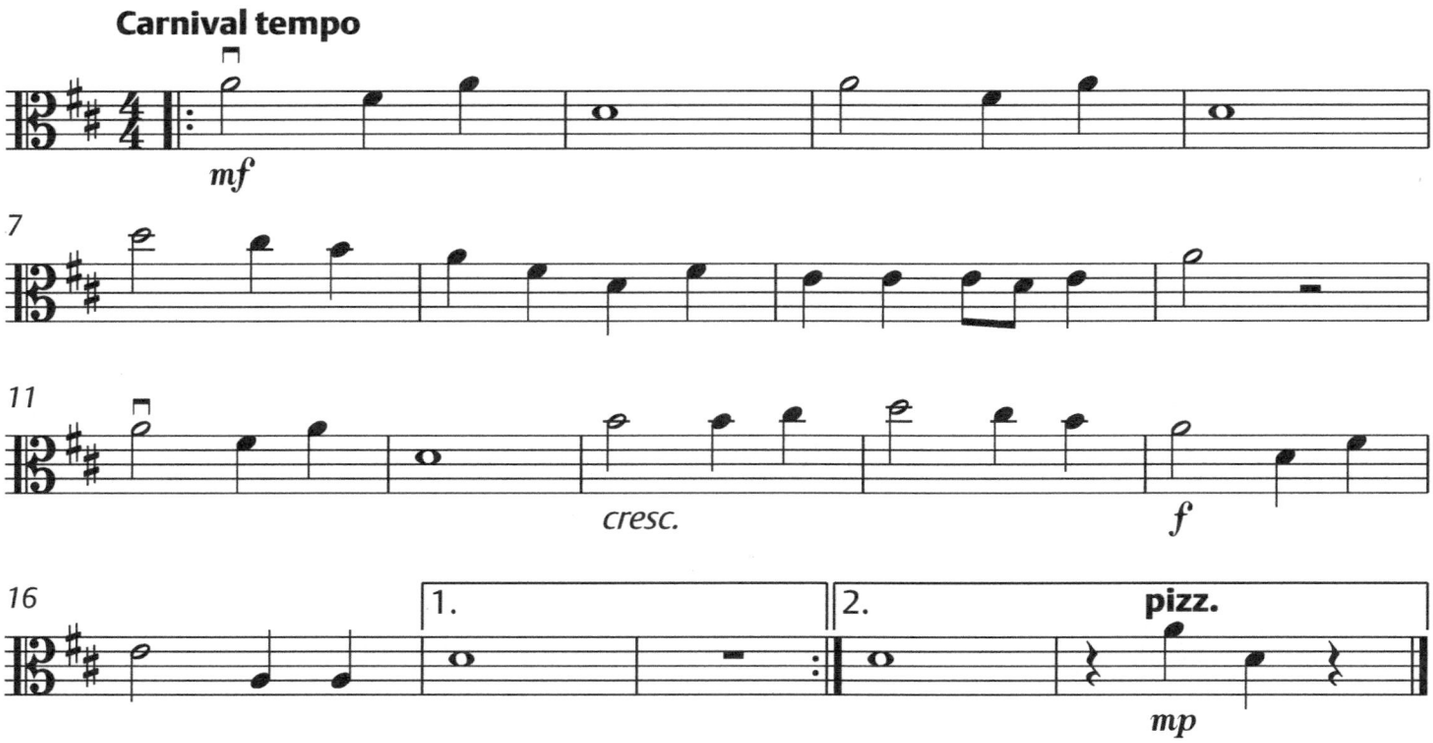

Now go back to page 13 and play the harder part of 'Ally bally'.

42. Calypso time—see page 34.

43. Tudor tune

C string special

KB & DB

44. Chopsticks for two

C string special

KB & DB

Now try the harder part of 'Copy cat' on page 10.

44. Rocky mountain—see page 34.

45. *Carrion crow*

American folk tune

Brightly

f

f

5

p

p

9

4

f

f

p

p

13

mf

mf

rit.

Try the harder part of 'Two in a boat' and 'London Bridge' on page 7.

45. Carrion crow—see page 35.

46. *Flying high*

KB & DB

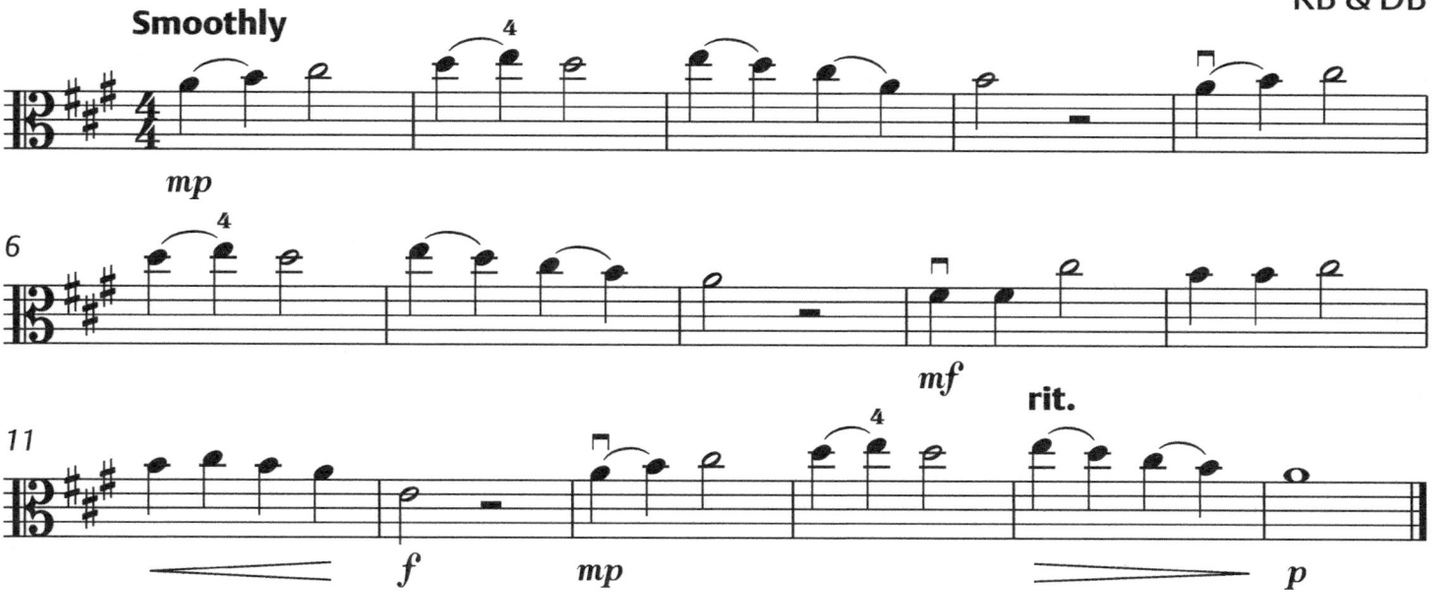

(No. 46 is not compatible with *Fiddle Time Joggers*.)

47. *Viola Time*

Count 4 bars

KB & DB

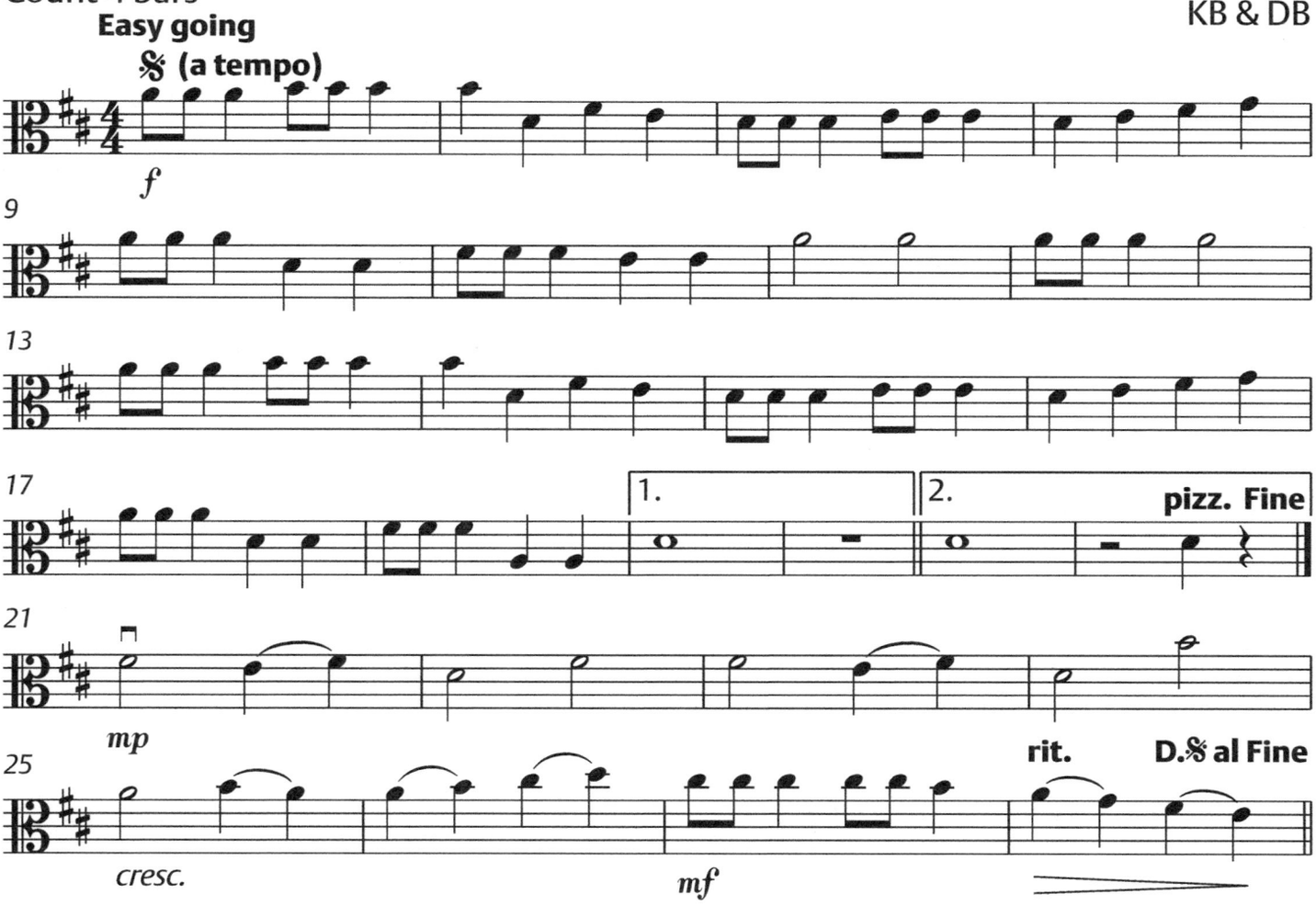

47. *Fiddle Time*—see page 35.

Ensemble parts

These additional parts are compatible with, and are numbered as, the pieces in *Fiddle Time Joggers.*

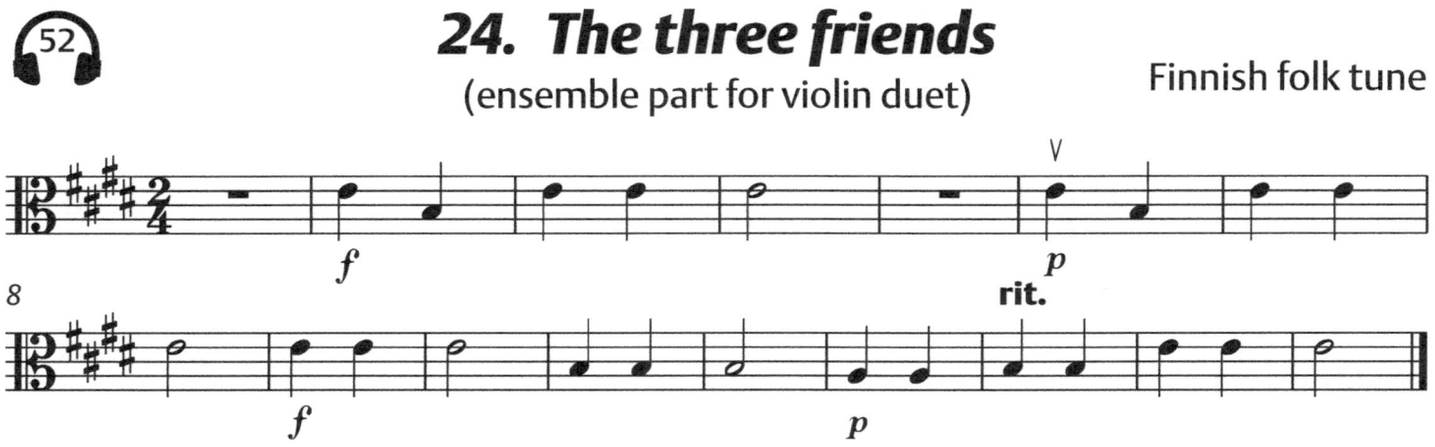

35. In the groove

Count 2 bars

(ensemble part)

KB & DB

Swing

mf cresc.

7

f

mf cresc.

11

15

f

20

rit.

mp

39. The old castle

(ensemble part)

KB & DB

With a singing tone

mp

5

9

mf

13

rit.

mp

p

42. Calypso time

(ensemble part)

Count 6 bars

KB & DB

Carnival tempo

mf

11

15

cresc.

19

f

1.

2.

pizz.

mp

Say this rhythm before you start to play:

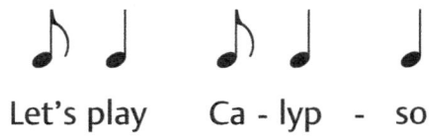

44. Rocky mountain

(lower part of violin duet)

American folk tune

Lively

f

mf

6

11

16

f

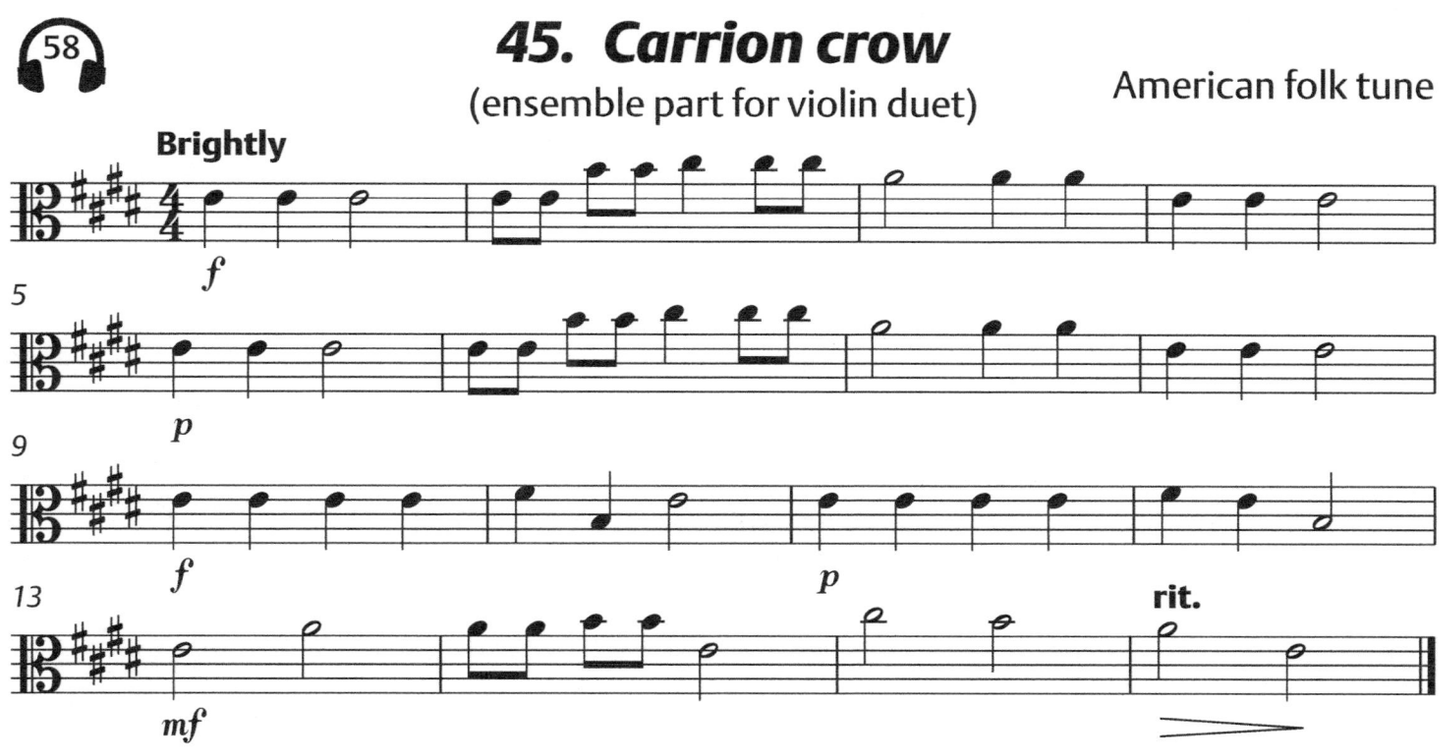
58
45. Carrion crow
(ensemble part for violin duet)
American folk tune
Brightly
f
5
p
9
f
p
13
rit.
mf

59
47. Fiddle Time
Count 4 bars
(ensemble part)
Easy going
KB & DB
(arco) (a tempo)
f
9
13
17
1.
2.
pizz. Fine
21
pizz.
mp
25
rit.
D.S. al Fine
cresc.
mf

Music Fact-Finder Page

Here are some of the words and signs you will find in some of your pieces!

How to play it

pizzicato or pizz. = pluck
arco = with the bow
⊓ = down bow
V = up bow
> = accent
𝅘𝅥𝅯 = tremolo

Don't get lost!

𝄆 𝄇 = repeat marks

1. 2. = first and second time bars
D.C. al Fine = repeat from the beginning and stop at **Fine**
D.𝄋 al Fine = repeat from the sign 𝄋 and stop at **Fine**
rit. = gradually getting slower
a tempo = back to the first speed
𝄐 = pause

Volume control

p (*piano*) = quiet
mp (*mezzo-piano*) = moderately quiet
mf (*mezzo-forte*) = moderately loud
f (*forte*) = loud
ff (*fortissimo*) = very loud
 or *crescendo* (*cresc.*) = getting gradually louder
 or *diminuendo* (*dim.*) = getting gradually quieter